The Creator's Gift

Roxanne August

TEACH Services, Inc.
PUBLISHING
www.TEACHServices.com ● (800) 367-1844

Copyright © 2020 Roxanne August

Copyright © 2020 TEACH Services, Inc.

ISBN-13: 978-1-4796-1216-1 (Paperback

ISBN-13: 978-1-4796- 1217-8 (ePub)

Library of Congress Control Number: 2020907525

TEACH Services, Inc.
PUBLISHING
www.TEACHServices.com • (800) 367-1844

I want you to love Jesus,

To know the joy that He brings.

The blessings He gives us,

And all the beautiful things.

The lofty mountains …

The wide-open seas.

The beautiful, blue sky …

The tall, stately trees.

The colorful fish …

The amazing birds, too!

He created these things,

And He shares them with you.

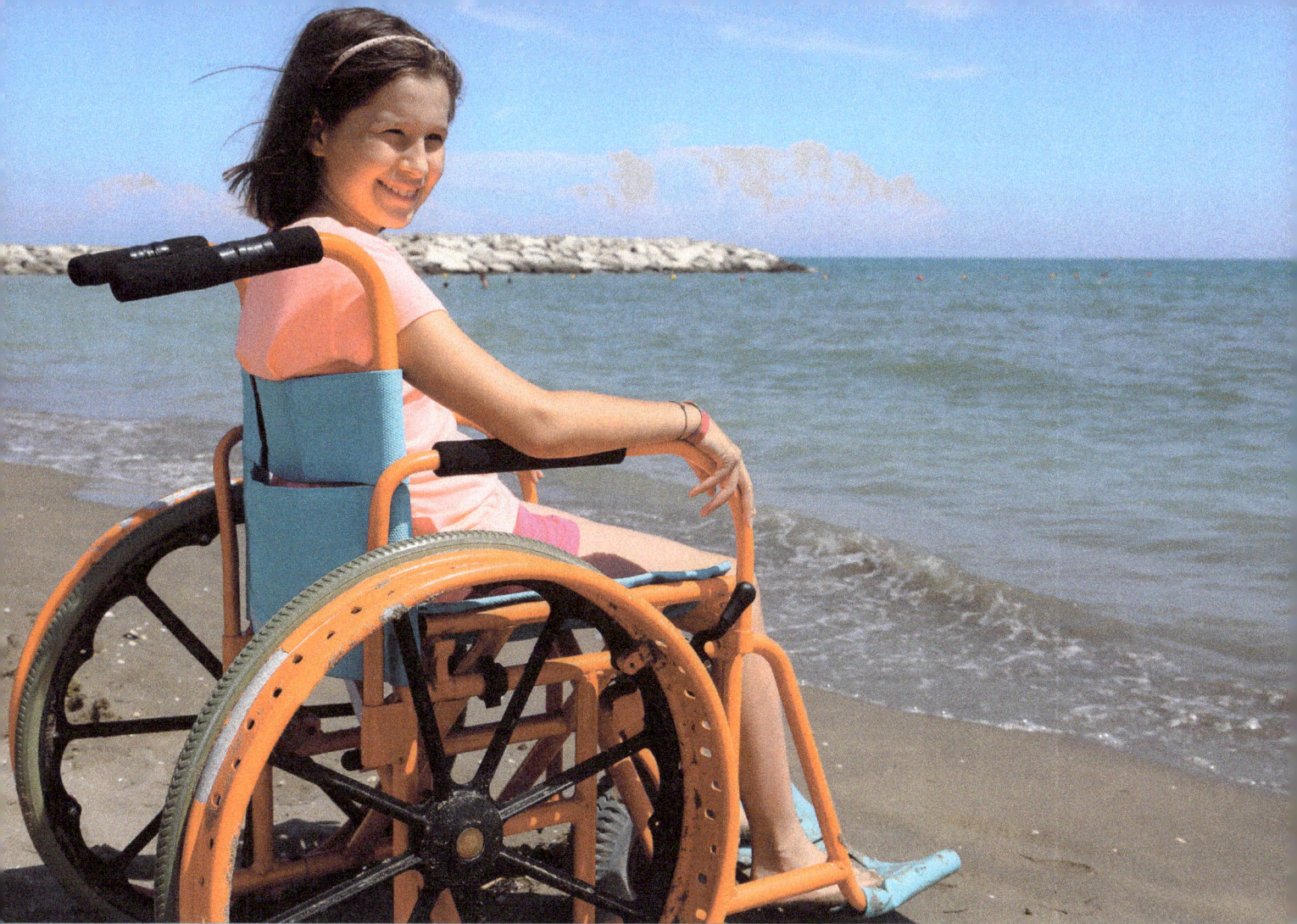

Believe it or not,

He didn't stop there!

There was something else

He wanted to share.

He gave you this gift,

One of His best!

And it is called

The Sabbath-day rest.

A day so special,
He set it apart...

For Him and for you,
To meet heart-to-heart.

www.ingramcontent.com/pod-product-compliance
Lightning Source LLC
Chambersburg PA
CBHW061417090426
42742CB00026B/3491